THE FLYING WINGS
of JACK NORTHROP

A Photo Chronicle

Garry R. Pape

with John M. Campbell & Donna Campbell

Schiffer Military/Aviation History
Atglen, PA

Acknowledgements

We would like to thank the many people who helped in the research and assisted in the production of this work. A number of past Northrop employees have given invaluable assistance. Roy Wolford, who was chief photographer during the time of the Wings, has graciously opened his photo files to us and provided much of what is in this publication. Past corporate historian Dr. Ira Chart was also kind enough to take us under his wing, and provided material assistance in the form of photographs and data, and provided needed encouragement and guidance in the early days of this effort. Good friend and fellow Wing enthusiast Robert Gerhart also opened his files to us and has given much appreciated assistance in our research efforts. Dan Hagedorn at the Smithsonian's National Air & Space Museum's archives division and Ray Wagner at the San Diego Aerospace Museum's archives have also given us much of their time and have greatly aided us in our research. We would also like to thank Terry Clawson at Northrop Corporation headquarters Public Information, and Bill Vas of the Northrop Vintage Aircraft Booster Club for their assistance in obtaining photos and drawings. Good friend and fellow aero enthusiast Gerry Balzer was his usual generous self and lent great assistance in our research.

First Edition
Copyright © 1994 by Garry R. Pape, John M. Campbell and Donna Campbell.

Library of Congress Catalog Number: 93-87470

Designed by Robert Biondi
ISBN: 978-0-88740-597-6
Printed in China

Introduction

This photo survey covers the flying wing and tailless craft designed and produced by Jack Northrop and his team at Northrop Aircraft, Incorporated between 1939 and the early 1950s. It is not meant to be a history in the usual sense, but to provide visual images which we hope the wing enthusiast, historian, or modeler would enjoy and perhaps find useful in their endeavors.

John K. "Jack" Northrop formed his 1939 company with the desire that his dream of a clean aircraft could come to fruition. To Jack Northrop, the wing, with its much reduced drag and increased lift, seemed to be "the" flying machine. His first effort, project N-1, would prove the wing could fly. Within a few years Jack's dream seemed to be on the verge of fulfillment when his company was awarded the contract for the large B-35 flying wing bomber project. Design, supply, and personnel problems would delay the project. Once airborne, the problems continued. The jet era had arrived and the engineers at Northrop readily converted the flying wing bomber into the jet-propelled YB-49. Once again Jack Northrop's dream seemed on the verge of being realized. But there were other technical problems. Politics and a rapid downsizing of the American air force with the conclusion of World War II were being felt at Northrop.

In the late 1940s and on, speed was of the essence in bombers. The Flying Wing was not built for speed. With two YB-49s destroyed by accident, the project was soon canceled and Jack Northrop left the aircraft industry. It would take years, but technology and the inherent attributes of a large flying wing bomber would converge in the late 1970s. Jack Northrop would be vindicated, and he would live long enough to learn of this fact – much sooner than most of the rest of the world.

This book is dedicated to the memory of John K. Northrop.

Contents

N-1M

John K. "Jack" Northrop established Northrop Aircraft, Inc. in 1939 with one purpose in mind, to finally build his flying wing. Not surprising, the new company's first project (N-1) was that of a flying wing. This craft was to be a flying laboratory, therefore it was considered a "flying mockup" and was given the designation of N-1M. Its purpose was to prove that a flying wing would fly. It was also used as a stepping stone to larger and more advanced versions of the flying wing.

This craft was of wooden construction which lent itself relatively easily to accomplished configuration changes thus enabling Northrop to vary sweepback, dihedral, and wing tip droop during the flight test program. The skin was basically mahogany with spruce and mahogany structural members. Metal was used only where absolutely required.

N-1M Statistics

Northrop Specification:	NS-1
Number Produced and Flown:	1
Civilian Registration:	NX-28311
Military Serial No.:	None
Wingspan:	38.72 ft. with dreop
Overall Length:	17.9 ft.
Overall Height	
Top of Canopy:	4.92 (without "hat")
Wing Area:	300 sq. ft.
Takeoff Weight:	3,900 lb.
Speed - Maximum:	200 mph
Speed - Cruising:	160 mph
Range:	300 miles
Service Ceiling:	4,000 ft.
Engines (original):	2 Lycoming O-146
(replacement):	2 Franklin 6AC264F2

This shot affords us a detailed closeup of the upper surface of the split flap rudders and the ground-adjustable drooped wing tip on the N-1M. (Wolford Collection)

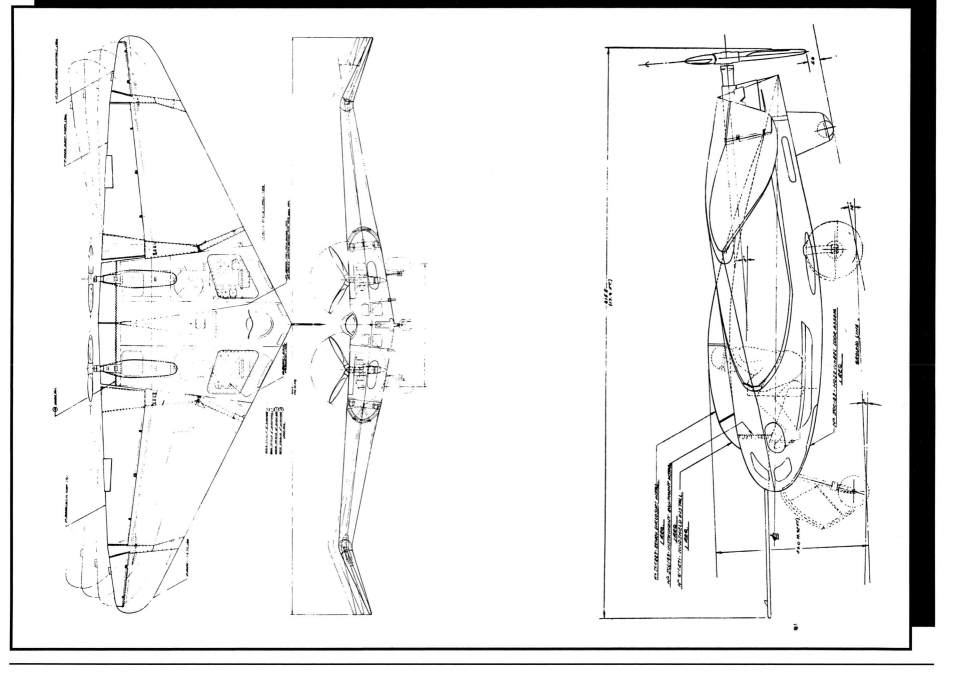

"Stripes" outboard of the engines are metal strips that cover the joint at which wing sweepback and dihedral could be adjusted on the ground. The N-1M is seen on one of the dry lakes near Muroc, in the southern part of the Mojave Desert in California, July 1941. (Wolford Collection)

Dr. Theodore von Karman, who was the director of the California Institute of Technology's Guggenheim School of Aeronautics, served as a consultant for the new Northrop Aircraft, Incorporated and influenced the design of the bird-like N-1M Jeep greatly. (Wolford Collection)

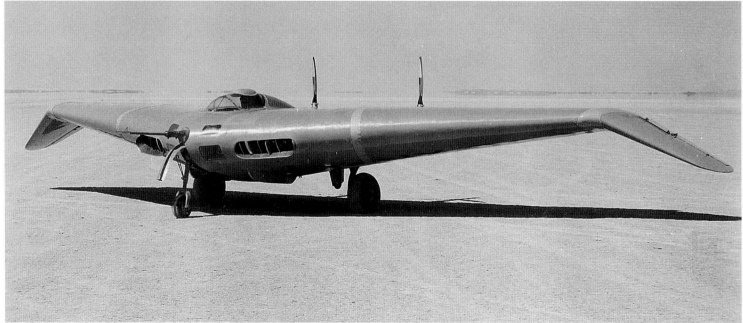

The N-1M flew most of its life with 117 h.p. Franklin engines and three-bladed propellers. Though considered quite under-powered, this configuration was an improvement over the original 65 h.p. Lycoming engines and two-bladed propeller combination. (Wolford Collection)

The N-1M's controls were similar to those used by European designers of flying wing type craft, including Germany's Horten brothers. Here the elevons running along the Jeep's trailing edge from just outboard of the engines to the wing tip break point are clearly visible. (Wolford Collection)

The metal "hat" on the top of the canopy was added early on to provide greater clearance for the pilot's head. (Wolford Collection)

Below: The N-1M is on truck scales being weighed on the desert floor near Muroc, California. Details of the engine intake, wing split cover, and main gear are shown in this close-up. (Wolford Collection)

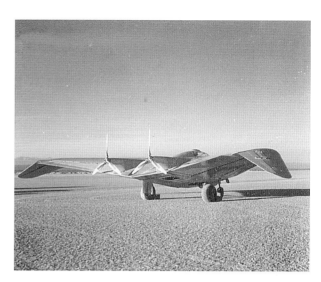

In this right rear view of the N-1M, the trim flaps are visible along the trailing edge between the engines. (Northrop)

Left: The chrome yellow N-1M was a company funded project and thus carried civil registration. It carried its black "NX-28311" until shortly after the XB-35 contract. At that time the N-1M flight test program became part of the XB-35 project. Sometime after this the national insignia was painted on the top and bottom of both right and left wing. In this photo the civil registration is quite visible in its vertical arrangement on the tail wheel cover. (Wolford Collection)

Corporate secretary and chief test pilot Moye Stephens takes the Jeep into the air. Because this 4,000 lb. flying wing was quite underpowered Jack Northrop contemplated changing the engines for a second time. (Wolford Collection)

A fixed tail wheel on the N-1M was carried to prevent excessive rollback when on the ground and to provide some directional stability. It also served to protect the propeller if a tail-low landing was made. (Wolford Collection)

The outer wing panel is at a greater sweep angle than the leading edge of the center wing section on this flight. (Wolford Collection)

Looking somewhat like Quetzalcoatlus northropi, the N-1M dromes across the desert. (Wolford Collection)

By the end of 1941 Northrop and his test crew found that the optional wing configuration was with no droop. (Wolford Collection)

Moye Stephens makes a low pass for the press on Photo Day. The news reel shorts at the movies would show the plane of the future to an awestruck public. (Wolford Collection)

Details concerning the existence of the N-1M appeared in both the U.S. and European press in mid-1941 much to the Air Corps dismay. On Thursday, December 4, 1941, under Army approval, Northrop held a Photo Day at Muroc. Soon the nation would have much more on its mind. (Wolford Collection)

Though the N-1M's performance was not outstanding, it did prove Jack Northrop's flying wing concept would fly and provided much from which the N-9Ms could profit. (Wolford Collection)

The N-1M flight test program concluded in early 1943. The aircraft went into storage at Northrop for a few months after which Northrop repainted it. The new paint scheme is seen in this and the following October 1943 photos prior to turning it over to the Army for future display. (Wolford Collection)

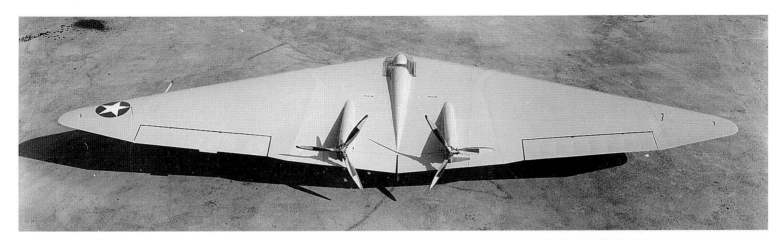

The yellow used in the refurbishment effort of the N-1M, was slightly different than the color originally used and the national insignia was applied only to the left top and right bottom wing surface. (Wolford Collection)

This craft has been restored by the Smithsonian's National Air and Space Museum and is on display. (Wolford Collection)

This aircraft went into storage status at Northrop shortly after this photo was taken in October 1943. In mid-1946 it went into temporary storage at Freeman Field in Indiana. It was eventually packed in two large boxes and remained in that status, rotting, for many years. In May 1979, restoration by the National Air & Space Museum in Silver Hill, Maryland commenced. It is today on display at that facility. (Wolford Collection)

N-9M

The N-9M was a research vehicle intended as an engineering tool to aid in the design and development of the B-35. Its construction was much like the N-1M and the four versions eventually built all differed from each other in control surfaces, radio, and electrical equipment. Like the N-1M, the N-9Ms were modified numerous time during their flight test program. As the engineering requirements for these craft decreased, they were pressed into a training role where both Northrop test pilots and Army Air Forces future would-be B-35 pilots received flying wing familiarization flight training.

N-9M Statistics:

Northrop Specification:	NS-99
Number Produced and Flown:	4 (designated N-9M [later referred to as the N-9M-1], N-9M-2, N-9MA, and N-9MB)
Civilian Registration:	None
Military Serial No.:	None
Wingspan:	
60.0 ft.	
Overall Length:	17.79 ft.
Overall Height	
Top of Canopy:	6.58 ft.
Top of Propeller:	8.65 ft.
Wing Area:	490 sq. ft.
Gross Weight:	6,326 lb.
Speed - Maximum:	258 mph
Speed - Cruising:	208 mph
Range:	500 miles
Service Ceiling:	19,500 ft.
Engines:	2 Menasco C6S-4 (first 3 N-9Ms) 2 Franklin O-540-7 (N-9MB)

Test pilot John Myers in the original N-9M over the southern California area in January 1943. Like its N-1M predecessor, the N-9M was painted overall chrome yellow. As other N-9Ms were produced, documents started referring to this one as the N-9M-1. (Wolford Collection)

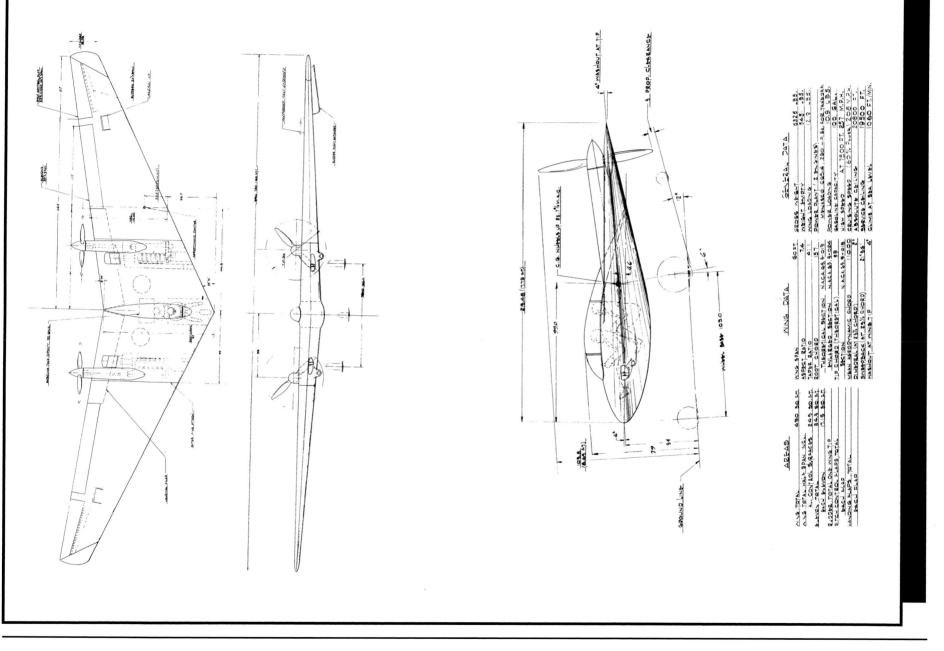

AREAS

WING, TOTAL	490 SQ.FT.
WING, TOTAL HALF SPAN, INCL.	
A.IL. CONTROL SURFACES	245 SQ.FT.
ELEVON, TOTAL	34.3 SQ.FT.
EACH ELEVON	17.15 SQ.FT.
RUDDER, TOTAL ONE WING TIP	
PITCH CONTROL FLAPS, TOTAL	
EACH FLAP	
LANDING FLAPS, TOTAL	
EACH FLAP	

WING DATA

WING SPAN	60 FT.
ASPECT RATIO	7.4
TAPER RATIO	4:1
ROOT CHORD	157
THEORETICAL SECTION	NACA 65,3-019
ENLARGED SECTION	NACA 65, 3-024
TIP CHORD (THEORETICAL)	39
SECTION	N ACA 65,3-018
MEAN AERODYNAMIC CHORD	110.0
DIHEDRAL (AT 25% CHORD)	0
SWEEPBACK (AT 25% CHORD)	21°44'
WASHOUT AT WING TIP	4°

GENERAL DATA

GROSS WEIGHT	6326 LBS.
WEIGHT EMPTY	5445 LBS.
WING LOADING	12.9 LBS.
POWER PLANT / 2 ENGINES	
MENASCO C6S4-4 290 -B.H.P. FOR TAKEOFF	
POWER LOADING	10.9 LBS.
GASOLINE CAPACITY	109 GAL.
HIGH SPEED AT 7500 FT. 257 M.P.H.	
CRUISING SPEED (60% POWER) 208 M.P.H.	
ABSOLUTE CEILING	21,500 FT.
SERVICE CEILING	19,500 FT.
CLIMB AT SEA LEVEL	1,060 FT./MIN.

N-9M flying mockup first flew on December 27, 1942. The diagonal line from intersection of wing tip and trailing edge across the wing to the leading edge is the wing tip rudder. The control devices were often referred to as split flap drag rudders. As this was war time and to show disdain toward the enemy, these devices were also referred to as "Jap Snappers" and teeth were painted on the inside surfaces. Moving from the wing tip inboard, other control devices included pitch control flaps, elevons, and landing flaps. The outboard wing sections also contained retractable ailerudder scoops on the upper surface and retractable rudder scoops on the surface. Just inboard of the engines are the exit flaps for engine cooling and exhaust. (Wolford Collection)

The N-9M, as part of a military project, did not carry a civilian registration. Because it was not considered an aircraft, but an engineering development tool, it also did not have a military serial number assigned to it. The national insignia was carried on the upper and lower wing surfaces of both the right and left wings as the N-1M did in its latter flight test period. Photo taken January 1943. (Wolford Collection)

N-9MA (on the left) and N-9MB (on the right) are seen in a hanger at Muroc. Control surfaces along the trailing edges of these two craft differed slightly from their two predecessors. From the wing tips in are the pitch trimmer (with a split drag rudder incorporated), elevon, and landing flap. At the leading edge the N-9MA had a fixed slot and the N-9MB had a closeable slot. (Wolford Collection)

Above: Northrop test pilot Max Stanley checks out Major Ritchie from Wright Field. By the time this photo was taken the upper surface of the N-9MA had been repainted blue. This was accomplished to aid ground observers in determining whether the craft was right side up or in the inverted position. (Wolford Collection)

Above: The N-9M-2 is pictured at Roach Dry Lake, Nevada. Originally it was constructed as an identical copy of the first N-9M. Later in its flight test, as shown in this photo, leading edge slats were added. Because of the unsatisfactory performance of the wing tip rudders on the N-9M, they were taped closed on the N-9M-2. (Wolford Collection)

Left: A close-up of the N-9M-2's canopy and cockpit area. (Wolford Collection)

Above: Last of the N-9M series, the N-9MB left the factory painted the standard chrome yellow on the upper surfaces and blue on the lower. The distinctive flight test boom usually sets the N-9MB apart from the other N-9Ms (the N-9M-2 flew with one for a short while). Photo taken October 1944. (USAF)

Left: Test pilot Max Stanley in the cockpit of the N-9MB. The antenna installed was quite different from the previous N-9Ms due to a change in radio equipment. (Northrop)

Right: Northrop test pilot Charles Fred Bretcher is checking out in the N-9MB. This photo gives a good view of the yellow and blue break line and of the boom installation. (Northrop)

The N-9MB was the only one of the N-9M series to be equipped with Franklin engines. Along with this engine change the air inlets were changed to an oblong design from the semi-circular air intakes of the earlier models. This craft is being restored by The Air Museum's Planes of Fame in Chino, California. (Wolford Collection)

A view from below shows the engine air intake of the Franklin engine powered N-9MB, and the separation of the blue and yellow paint scheme. (Northrop)

From left to right are: N-9MB (flight test boom identifies it), N-9MA, and the N-9M-2 (leading edge slat identifies it). Note the national markings on the N-9MB which has none on the bottom, the N-9MA marking is under the right wing, and the N-9M-2 marking is under the left wing. Photo taken February 1946. (Wolford Collection)

National insignia markings differ on the upper surfaces also. N-9MB (left background) and N-9MA (right background) both have the insignia on their upper left wing while the N-9M-2 has it on the upper right wing. When this photo was taken the N-9MA was still in its overall yellow paint scheme. (Wolford Collection)

This view of the cockpit installations of the N-9MB shows the cramped confines of the craft with every spare inch of space delegated to its specific instrument or control. (Wolford Collection)

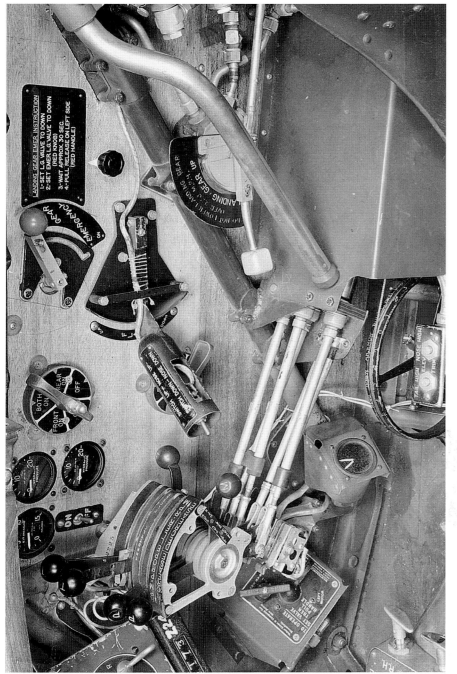

Above: This right side cockpit photo shows the throttle controls and wing trim on the N-9MB. Below: The left side cockpit photo shows the landing gear controls and radio in the N-9MB. (both - Wolford Collection)

XP-56

In 1939 the Army Air Corps was looking for a new pursuit plane. It was to advance the state of the art in fighter design and non-critical materials were to be used. Northrop was one of three companies selected to construct examples of its design. The Northrop XP-56 was constructed out of magnesium and was welded by the Northrop-developed heliarc welding process.

First XP-56, serial number 41-786, at Northrop Field in Hawthorne, California. This photo taken in April of 1943 shows it in two-tone upper surface and gray lower surfaces. The drooped wing tips were part of the same ideas as in the N-1M design. Control surfaces were much the same as the N-9M-1. (Northrop)

XP-56 Statistics:

Northrop Specification:	NS-2
Number Produced and Flown:	2
Military Serial Numbers:	41-786 and 42-38353
Wingspan:	42.57 ft.
Overall Length:	23.58 ft.
Overall Height:	9.75 (No. 1 XP-56)
Wing Area:	311 sq. ft.
Gross Weight:	11,350 lb.
Speed - Maximum:	467 mph (design goal, not attained)
Speed - Cruising:	375 mph (design goal, not attained)
Range:	450 miles
Service Ceiling:	33,000 ft.
Engines:	1 Pratt & Whitney R-2800-29
Armament (Proposed): and	4 - .50 cal. machine guns 2 - 20 mm cannon

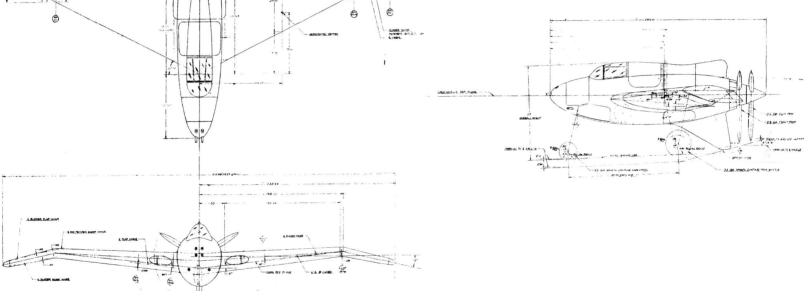

XP-56 No.1 going through engine check and warm-up. The air cooled Pratt & Whitney R-2800 required a special cooling system in this enclosed configuration. Blisters cover two of its six gun ports. (Northrop)

On Sept. 6, 1943, now painted silver, the XP-56 flew two of its four flights. That following October 8th, two additional flights were made. Following the second flight of that day, test pilot John Myers (shown in the cockpit) made a high speed taxi test. The left main tire blew causing the plane to tumble, curling itself into a heap of wreckage. Myers suffered a back injury. National insignia is outlined in red. (Northrop)

XP-56, No.2 serial number 42-38353. Wing tip opening is into a venturi through which air would freely flow during flight. A valve could be actuated by the pilot depressing the rudder pedals which would in turn direct the airflow to a bellows which would assist in operating the wing tip split flap rudders. (Northrop)

The paint scheme on the second XP-56 was olive drab upper surface and gray lower. The tip of the enlarged dorsal fin, which was later added to the No.1 XP-56 prior to its Oct. 1943 flight, was painted insignia yellow as were the serial numbers. (Wolford Collection)

This close-up reveals a good view of the exhaust stacks and the dual rotating propellers. The wheel added to the ventral fin was in lieu of skid on the first XP-56 to prevent it from digging into the ground in a tail low position. One can well imagine the fin digging into the ground in a tail-low position, as happened in John Myers' accident. (Wolford Collection)

Left: Armament for the XP-56 was intended to be four .50 cal. machine guns and two 20 mm cannons, although never installed. (Wolford Collection)

Right: The sleek XP-56 never achieved the performance once envisioned. With the emergence of the jet engine into the scheme of things, the XP-56 with its poor performance was soon put into storage. (Wolford Collection)

Gun blisters not included in the second XP-56. It is not clear from available records if the provision for the armament was entirely deleted from this craft. The close proximity of the vertical fin to the ground is clearly seen, as well as the overall paint scheme. (Northrop)

The second XP-56 has survived time and the smelters. This aircraft now sits at the Smithsonian's National Air and Space Museum storage facility at Silver Hill, Maryland, awaiting restoration by the competent staff at the Paul E. Garber facility. (USAF)

MX-324/334

Like the N-1M and N-9M, the MX-324 was a flying mockup for the XP-79 project, and was basically of wooden construction. As gliders, they carried the designation of MX-334 with a lower security classification which made the engineers and flight test people's work much easier. With its intended Aerojet rocket motor, it would revert back to its original designation of MX-324 with greater security requirements.

MX-324/334 Statistics:

Northrop Specification:	NS-12
Number Produced and Flown:	3 (3 as MX-334 gliders, one had Aerojet rocket installed and redesignated MX-324)
Civilian Registration:	None
Military Serial No.:	None
Wingspan:	32 ft.
Overall Length:	12 ft.
Overall Height:	7 ft. (with added on vertical)
Wing Area:	244 sq. ft.
Takeoff Weight:	2,500 lb. (about 3,000 lb. with rocket motor installed)
Speed - Maximum:	300 mph (with rocket motor)
Range:	25 miles
Service Ceiling:	
Engines:	Aerojet XCAL-200

As part of the XP-79 rocket-powered interceptor project, three proof-of-concept wood constructed flying mockups were to be constructed. These were given Materiel Command project number MX-324 and was a highly classified project. As unpowered gliders, they were given project number MX-334 and were of a lower classification. (Wolford Collection)

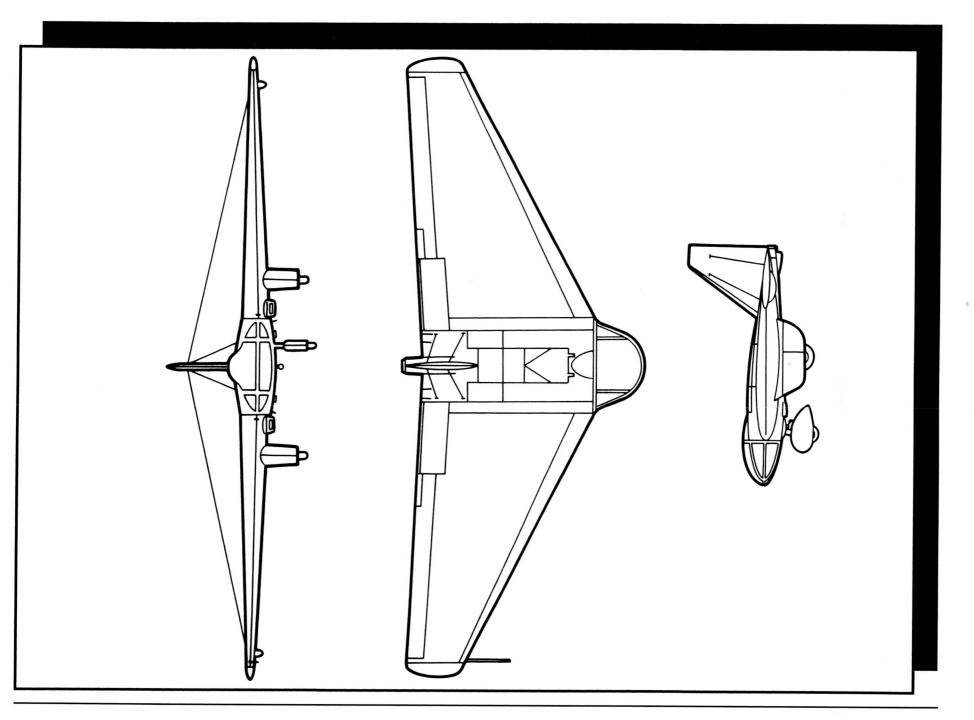

Originally envisioned as a pure flying wing, engineering calculations and wind tunnel results forced the Northrop design team to "scab" on a vertical fin. A number of fin designs were tried as can be seen by comparison of this photo to that on page 30. (Wolford Collection)

April 1944, a variety of skid and dolly combinations were also tried. Like the N-1M and N-9Ms, the MX-324/334 were painted chrome yellow. (Wolford Collection)

Like the N-9Ms, these craft were considered engineering development tools and did not have military serial numbers assigned yet still had national insignias applied. (Wolford)

The admiring onlookers and the Lockheed XP-49 bring into perspective the diminutive size of the MX-324/334 series craft. (Harold G. Martin photo, Kansas Aeronautical Historical Society Collection)

The pilot flew the MX-324/334 in prone position. A chin support is clearly visible in this detailed close-up. (Harold G. Martin photo, Kansas Aeronautical Historical Society Collection)

Possibly the MX-334 number 2, with a crudely applied set of wheel pants affixed to the landing gear. Even though it is reported that these craft never flew without a vertical fin, it is missing in this photo. Note: red wing tips and diagonal stripes have been added. (San Diego Aerospace Museum)

Third MX-334 on April 20, 1944. Very aerodynamic pants have been included with the fixed landing gear on this MX-334, which would become the only MX-324 once the Aerojet rocket motor was installed. (Wolford Collection)

This head-on view shows the aircraft's low stance to the ground. On each side of the canopy are the tow cable attachment points. A P-38 was used to tow these ships into the air. (Wolford Collection)

The control surface and fin bracing cables are shown in this rear view. The booted main gear and nose gear are also visible. (Wolford Collection)

Northrop Test Pilot Harry Crosby as seen here ready to be pulled into the wild blue yonder over the Mojave Desert. The tow cable connecting the P-38 tow ship to the MX-334 is clearly seen angling down from the cockpit. (Wolford Collection)

XP-79B

Jack Northrop was always ready to apply the flying wing concept to any opportunity that might arise. The XP-79 was to be a rocket-powered interceptor constructed out of non-critical war material. Like the XP-56, Northrop chose magnesium. Because of developmental problems with the proposed 2,000 lb. thrust rocket motor being developed by Aerojet that was scheduled for this airplane, the powerplant was changed and two Westinghouse turbojets were installed in the sole example produced, the XP-79B.

The thick magnesium construction and internal armor plate along the leading edge to protect the fuel tanks was never intended for ramming, contrary to P.R. touting such operations. The XP-79B incorporated the same wing-tip inlets for bellows-type rudder controls as in the second XP-56. (Wolford Collection)

The twin rudders must have grieved Jack Northrop greatly. With the pilot flying the aircraft in the prone position, it was impossible to place the nose gear on the center line of the nose area. The retractable quadricycle gear was the answer. (Wolford Collection)

XP-79B Statistics:

Northrop Specification:	NS-14
Number Produced and Flown:	1
Military Serial Number:	43-52437
Wingspan:	38 ft.
Overall Length:	14 ft.
Overall Height:	7 ft.
Wing Area:	278 sq. ft.
Takeoff Weight:	8,669 lb.
Speed - Maximum:	547 mph
Speed - Cruising:	480 mph
Range:	993 miles
Service Ceiling:	40,000 ft.
Engines:	2 Westinghouse 19-B
Armament (Proposed):	Four .50 cal. machine guns

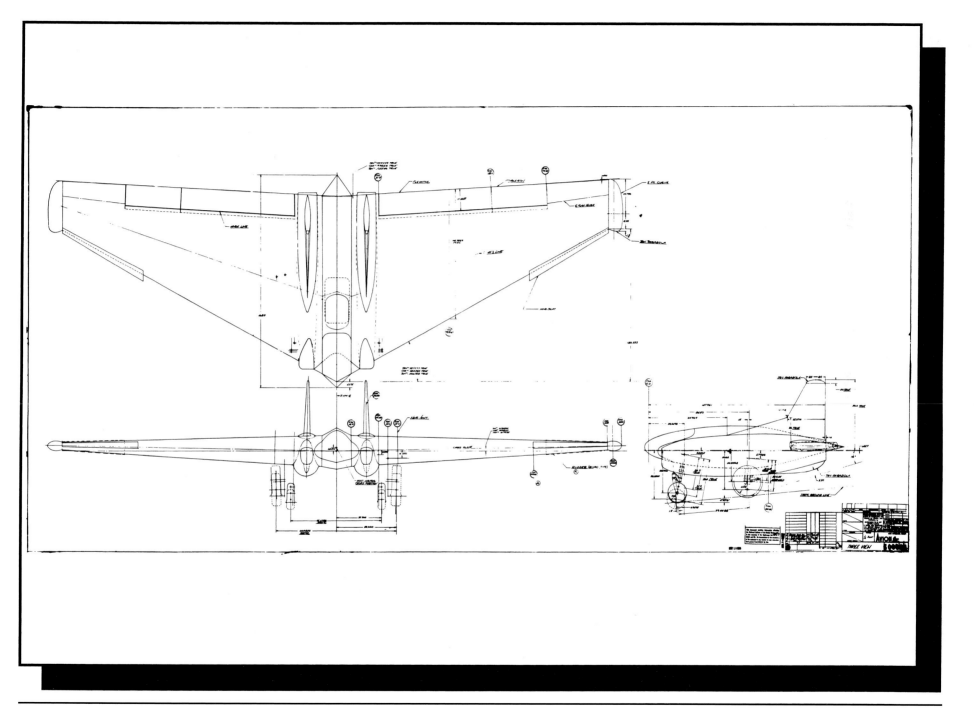

Left: Closeup of the XP-79B's nose gear. (Wolford Collection)

Right: Slightly larger main, or aft, gear of the XP-79B. Because of the unfortunate accident during the plane's first flight, landing with the unique quadricycle gear was never accomplished. (Wolford Collection)

XP-79B up on jack stands gives some indication of what the gunner in an enemy bomber would be looking at as the speedy little interceptor swooped down upon him. This shot also gives a good look at the cramped pilot's quarters as well as showing the large intakes for the two Westinghouse 19-B engines. (Wolford)

Initially designed to be rocket powered, Aerojet's developmental problems brought about the change to a pair of turbojet engines. Unfortunately, the XP-79B's first flight was it's last. (Wolford)

JB-1/10

Germany's V-1 flying bombs impressed the US Army Air Forces and a call went out for an American version. Northrop stepped up and offered a version which was developed largely from the MX-324/334 program. Originally 13 JB-1s were ordered. But only two were built; one as a glider which was used in the flight test program and one powered by GE jet engines. The remainder of the order were completed as JB-10s which were powered by a Ford Motor Company pulse jet engine.

JB-1 and JB-10 Statistics:

	Overall	JB-1	JB-10
Northrop Specification:	NS-16		
Number Produced and Flown:	12		
Wingspan:		28.33 ft.	29.08 ft.
Overall Length:		10.5 ft.	11.83 ft.
Overall Height:		4.5 ft.	4.83 ft.
Wing Area:		155 sq.ft	163 sq ft
Launch Weight:		7,080 lb.	7,084 lb
Speed - Launch:		160 mph	220 mph
Speed - Cruising:		427 mph	426 mph
Range:		670 miles	185 miles
Engines:		2 G.E.	1 Ford
		Type B1	PJ-31-1
Armament:		Two 2,000 lb bombs	Two 1,825 lb warheads

The JB-1 was one of a series of pilotless craft designed to bring the United States into the "Robot" weapons race. Thirteen JB-1s were originally ordered but only two were built and flown; this one pictured and the other as a glider prototype. (Wolford Collection)

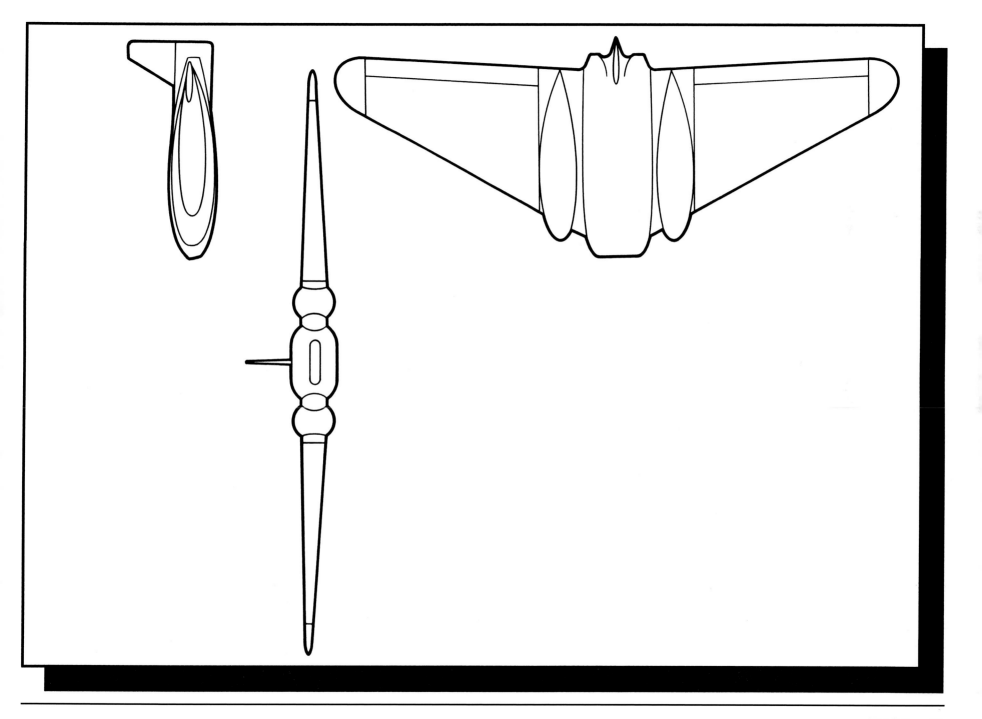

This glider variant of the JB-1 was constructed to prove and demonstrate its flying qualities. Like the MX-334 gliders, it too was towed into the air by a P-38. The pods on either side of the main body of the craft were built to house a 2,000 lb. bomb. (Wolford Collection)

Known to most of those who worked on this craft as Project 16, the glider is here seen in September 1944. The landing gear on the glider were hard mounted and quite a thrill for the pilot as it slammed down on the desert floor upon landing. (Wolford Collection)

Rear view of the JB-1 Glider. Often this glider has been referred to as the JB-1A, but the JB-10 also carried that designation for a time. Apparently the "A" was a Northrop engineering designation and not an official military designation. (Wolford Collection)

14329-045 NORTHROP
FRONT LEFT 3/4 LOW VIEW
JB-1A

The JB-10 was basically the JB-1 with a "Ford" Motor Company version of the infamous German V-1s Fiesler pulse jet engine. Ten of the eleven JB-10s produced were test flown. (Wolford Collection)

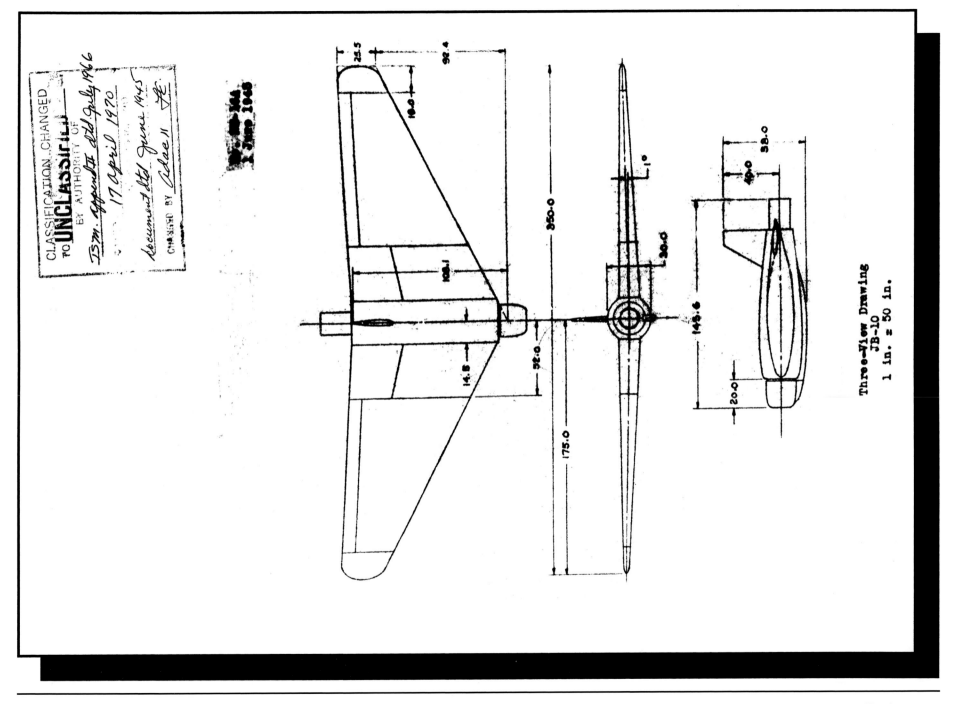

Three-View Drawing
JB-10
1 in. = 50 in.

XB/YB-35

The B-35 seemed to be Jack Northrop's dream of a flying wing come true. It was designed to meet the need for an intercontinental bomber capable of hitting German targets from the US. Requirements called for this mammoth wing to carry a bomb load of 10,000 pounds with a range of 10,000 miles. Orders of two experimental, 13 service test, and 200 production were once on Northrop's books. But a lack of engineers and manufacturing space as well as problems with associate contractors and government furnished equipment (such as engines and associated equipment) caused the development schedule to slip to where the production order was canceled. Eventually only three B-35 variants would take to the air with continuing powerplant related problems during flight test and jet engine development, the propeller driven B-35 gave place to the jet powered B-49.

XB/YB-35 Statistics:

Northrop Specification:	NS-9
Number Produced and Flown:	Two XB-35s & One YB-35
Military Serial Numbers:	42-13603, 42-38323, & 42-102366
Wingspan:	172 ft.
Overall Length:	53.08 ft.
Overall Height:	20 ft.
Wing Area:	4,000 sq. ft.
Takeoff Weight:	162,000 lb.
Speed - Maximum:	391 mph
Speed - Cruising:	240 mph
Range:	7,500 miles
Service Ceiling:	40,000 ft.
Engines:	4 Pratt & Whitney R-4360 2 each of the -17 and the -21.
Bomb Load:	52,200 lb. max.
Armament:	Turrets with .50 cal. machine guns. One turret, upper and lower outboard wing with two guns each, one upper and lower center line turret with four guns each, and a tail stinger with four guns.

The first XB-35, serial number 42-13603, as it approaches readiness for its first taxi tests in April 1946. It is seen without its final finish, details such as simulated gun blisters, antennas, astrodome, and canopy shown in clear detail. Of interest is the six bladed counter-rotating propellers on the left outboard engine. Apparently this engine-propeller combination was only ground tested. (Northrop)

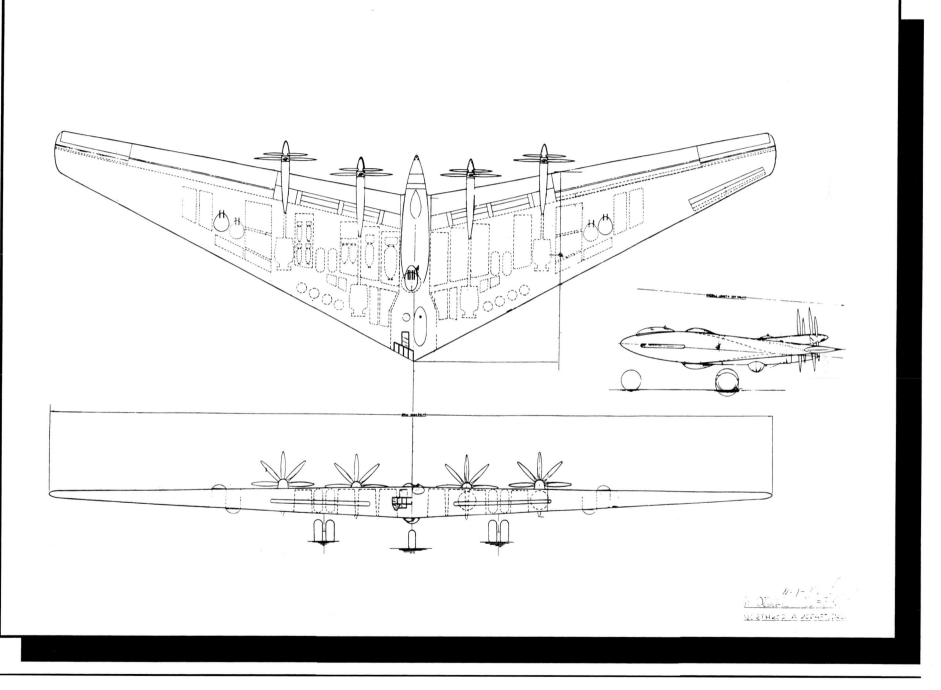

Above: XB-35, serial number 42-13603 during engine run-up tests in April 1946. At one time two experimental, 13 service test, and 200 production flying wing bombers were on order. Only six would take to the air and others would be mostly assembled by the time the project was canceled. (Northrop)

Above right: The XB-35 was clearly the main attraction at Northrop's Open House Celebration in May of 1946. The control and upper wing surfaces are quite detailed here and the similarity to the N-9MB is also apparent. (Campbell Archives)

Right: XB-35 No.1 towers over the admiring onlookers again at the Northrop open house. A large portion of the leading edge of the wing was part of the engine air intake and cooling system. (Northrop)

OPPOSITE: Arranged in a somewhat unconventional manner, switches and conventional instruments were mounted between the two pilot stations. The throttle controls are suspended from the overhead as was the case in Navy flying boats such as the Catalina. Radio, fuel, and air speed gauges mounted in the centerline console between the pilot stations. The co-pilot had only limited control of the aircraft and could neither takeoff nor land the aircraft. (Northrop)

Above: It might have seemed that Jack Northrop's dream was being realized as the XB-35 rolled down the Northrop Field runway on June 25, 1946. But the engine drive shaft, gear box, and propellers that had helped to delay the program would eventually spell the end of the XB-35 project. Time too, was not kind, as during the extended development program the jet engine became a practical means of propulsion. (Northrop)

Right: XB-35 as seen just prior to taxi tests in May 1946. Split-flap rudders attached to the pitch trimmers, landing flaps, and elevrons are along the trailing edge. Automatic wing slot is visible just to the rear of the leading edge of the port side. (Campbell Archives)

Above: First flight of the XB-35 was on June 25, 1946. The scimitar-like craft is seen here at the beginning of a nearly uneventful 44 minute flight from Hawthorne to Muroc. (Campbell Archives)

Below: XB-35, serial number 42-13603. Test pilot Max Stanley commented after his first flight in the XB-35 that he wouldn't have known that he was in a flying wing had he not looked behind him. (Northrop)

The crew of the No.1 XB-35, Max R. Stanley pilot, left, flight engineer Orva H. Douglas center, and co-pilot Charles Fred Bretcher. When Stanley first joined the Northrop team, he requested not to be assigned to the flying wing project, thinking that it was beyond his skills. He soon learned differently and loved it. (Northrop)

Above: Front view of the second XB-35, serial number 42-38323. This airplane, as well as the sole YB-35 to fly, was equipped with gun turrets. Compare the leading edge engine air intakes to the change made in the YB-49's. (USAF) Below: The aerodynamic cleanness would never be realized in the B-35s, but the YB-49s would show what their potential was. (USAF)

Below: Rear view of the XB-35 on the flight ramp at Muroc. Flights were very limited due to gearbox, propeller, and other engine problems, including the cooling system. (USAF)

Only the pilot rode in the high seat. Co-pilot and bombardier rode at lower levels and to the right of the aircraft's center line. The pilots did not have any problem flying in their offset position to the left of the airplane's center line. (Northrop)

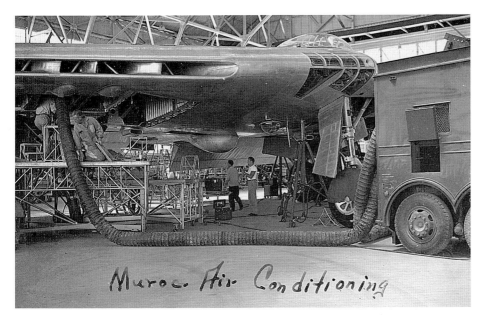

Above left: The first XB-35 in a Muroc hanger under maintenance. The partially disassembled condition provides some excellent views of the wing's construction. Aerodynamic blisters were used in lieu of turrets on this aircraft; the lower center turret position is quite visible in this photo. (Northrop)

Above: The XB-35s were plagued with propeller and gearbox problems. Though many engineering and test hours were expended, the problems were never resolved. In an effort to save the program, the dual rotating propeller system was replaced with a single-rotation four-bladed propeller and associated gearbox. (Northrop)

Left: Flight testing of the XB-35s was quite limited because of gearbox, propeller, and other engine problems. To add to Northrop's headaches, the auxiliary power units were quite troublesome as well. Most of this problem equipment was government furnished. (Northrop)

Because of the constant and seemingly unsolvable governor and other engine and propeller related problems, the counter rotating eight-bladed propellers on the two XB-35s were replaced with single rotating four-bladed propellers. Though this seemed to alleviate some of the engine/propeller problems, other problems arose and aircraft performance deteriorated drastically. (Northrop)

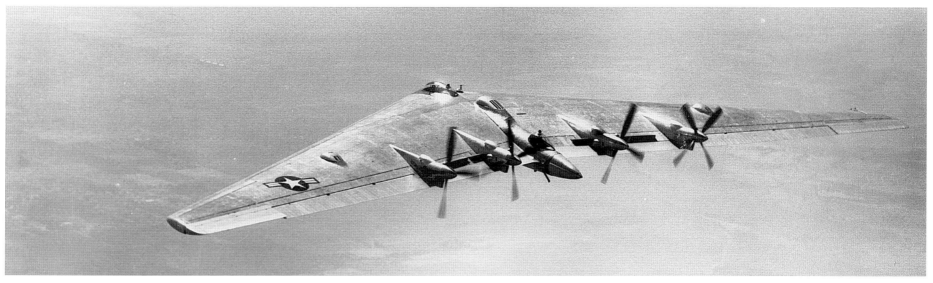

Above: The only YB-35, serial number 42-102366, to fly ended up being more of the XB-35 configuration. Because of the problems the two XB-35s were experiencing, the YB-35 had the single-rotating four-bladed propellers installed prior to maiden flight. (Northrop)

Below: Once in the air, the beauty of the XB-35 cutting through the sky was a wonder to behold. With the demise of the B-35 program, the first XB-35 had accomplished 19 flights and the second XB-35 recorded only 8 flights. Official records do not include the total flight history of the sole YB-35 to fly. (Northrop)

YB-49/YRB-49A

The B-49 was an outgrowth of the B-35 program. The three B-49 variants that did fly were modified YB-35 airframes. The YB-49s seemed to symbolize all that Jack Northrop could wish for. Most test pilots felt that these aircraft flew well, much like a fighter. But speed was a major requirement as the 1950s began and the flying wing was not built for speed. It would be some 30 years later before the inherent attributes of a flying wing would coincide with military requirements.

The first jet propelled YB-49, serial number 42-102367, nearing completion of its changeover from a propeller driven YB-35 airframe. In the background is the second YB-49, serial number 42-102368, undergoing the same conversion. (Northrop)

YB-49 and YRB-49A Statistics:

Northrop Specification:	NS-9 (YB-49) and NS-41 (YRB-49A)
Number Produced and Flown:	Two YB-49s & One YRB-49A
Military Serial Numbers:	42-102367, 42-102368, & 42-102376
Wingspan:	172 ft.
Overall Length:	53.08 ft.
Overall Height:	15.17 ft. (20.0 ft. YRB-49A)
Wing Area:	4,000 sq. ft.
Takeoff Weight:	193,938 lb. (175,000 lb.)
Speed - Maximum:	493 mph (440 mph)
Speed - Cruising:	419 mph (392 mph)
Range:	3,155 miles (2,625 miles)
Service Ceiling:	40,700 ft. (42,600 ft.)
Engines:	8 Allison J-35-A-15 (6 Allison J-35-A-19)
Bomb Load:	32,000 lb. max. (six 188 lb. T-89 Flash Bombs)
Armament:	Tail stinger with four .50 cal. machine guns. (None on YRB-49A)

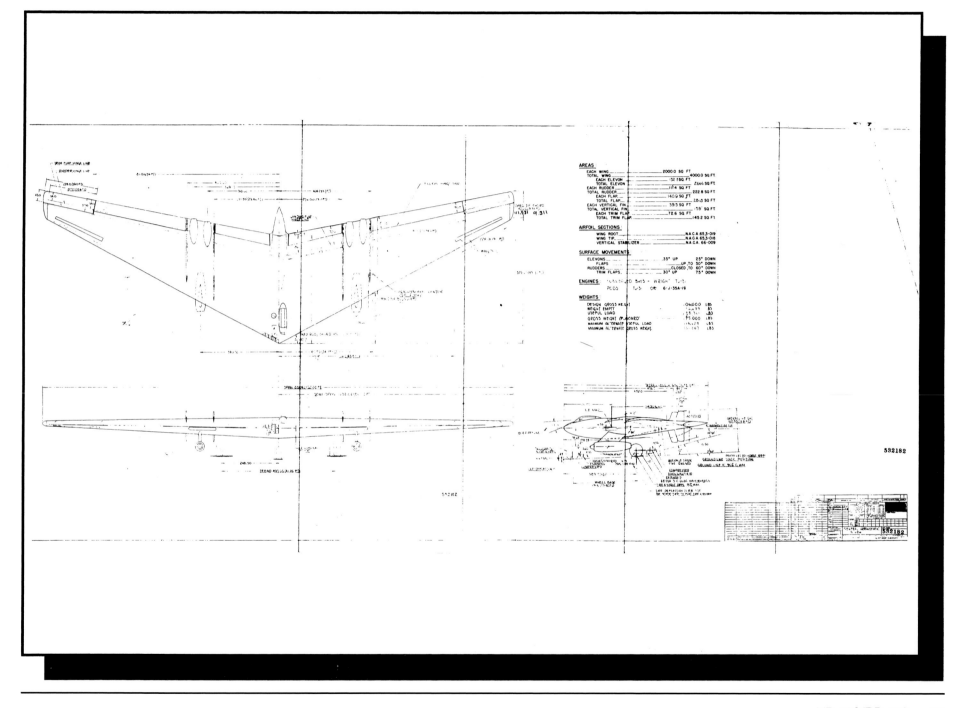

AREAS
EACH WING .... 2000.0 SQ FT
TOTAL WING .... 4000.0 SQ FT
EACH ELEVON .... 132.3 SQ FT
TOTAL ELEVON .... 264.6 SQ FT
EACH RUDDER .... 111.4 SQ FT
TOTAL RUDDER .... 222.8 SQ FT
EACH FLAP .... 140.9 SQ FT
TOTAL FLAP .... 281.8 SQ FT
EACH VERTICAL FIN .... 39.5 SQ FT
TOTAL VERTICAL FIN .... 158 SQ FT
EACH TRIM FLAP .... 72.6 SQ FT
TOTAL TRIM FLAP .... 145.2 SQ FT

AIRFOIL SECTIONS
WING ROOT .... N.A.C.A 65,3-019
WING TIP .... N.A.C.A 65,3-018
VERTICAL STABILIZER .... N.A.C.A. 66-009

SURFACE MOVEMENTS
ELEVONS .... 35° UP   25° DOWN
FLAPS .... UP TO 50° DOWN
RUDDERS .... CLOSED TO 60° DOWN
TRIM FLAPS .... 30° UP   75° DOWN

ENGINES   INSTALLED 3413 - WRIGHT   TG-31
          PODS   TG-31   OR   6-J-35A-19

WEIGHTS
DESIGN GROSS WEIGHT .... 104,000 LBS
WEIGHT EMPTY .... 74,939 LBS
USEFUL LOAD .... 55,311 LBS
GROSS WEIGHT (PLACARD) .... 95,000 LBS
MAXIMUM ALTERNATE USEFUL LOAD .... 143,629 LBS
MAXIMUM ALTERNATE GROSS WEIGHT .... 193,667 LBS

532182

Above: The first YB-49 was actually the modification of the second YB-35. Changing from reciprocating to jet engines added some 30,000 pounds to the aircraft's weight, decreasing the bomb load (bomb bay change due to jet engine installation) by 12,800 pounds and decreased its range to about 4,900 miles. (Northrop)

Below: Much to Jack Northrop and his engineers dislike, small vertical fins had to be added to the YB-49 for stability. The fins did not dampen out oscillations as well as the propellers did on the XB-35. Still a beauty to the eye, it was a pleasure to fly, much unlike the XB-35. Handling characteristics were more like a fighter than a big bomber. (Northrop)

Stanley, Bretcher, and Douglas take the YB-49 into the air for its first flight on Sept. 29, 1947. Locals from Hawthorne look on from behind the fence that separated them from Northrop Field. (Northrop)

The bombardier's station pictured here is pretty self-explanatory. The switches, circuit breakers, and radio channel selectors all appear to be similar to the other compartmentalized stations. To the left in the photo, which is the aircraft's leading edge, is the window that the bombardier used to aim. (Northrop)

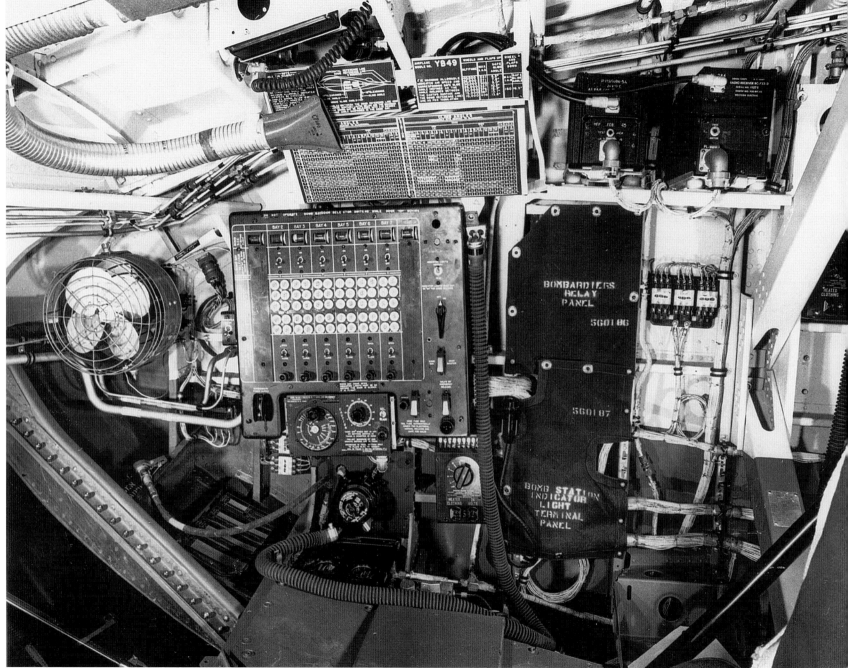

The flight engineer's station, depicting the many temperature, flow and capacity gauges. Fuel as in all aircraft was kept as evenly balanced as possible, with more attention being paid to trim and engine power settings in order to maintain clean flight characteristics. (Northrop)

In the air most pilots heaped praises on the flying qualities of the jet powered flying wing. But to the bombardier it was an entirely different story. Technology had to advance somewhat before it was an acceptable bombing platform. Oscillation problems had to wait for stability augmentation technology to catch up. (Northrop)

The slim silhouette gives some indication of the inherent "stealthiness" of the YB-49. On a number of occasions as the YB-49 penetrated the air space around the Half Moon Bay area along the California coast, radar failed to pick it up. (Northrop)

When the big flying wing converted from being a prop-driven bomber to jet power, the landing gear door design was not reexamined. It turned out that the door retraction speed was not great enough to prevent damage caused by the higher speeds the jet engines gave the bomber. To prevent damage, the pilots had to put the plane in a steep climb angle immediately after takeoff. (Northrop)

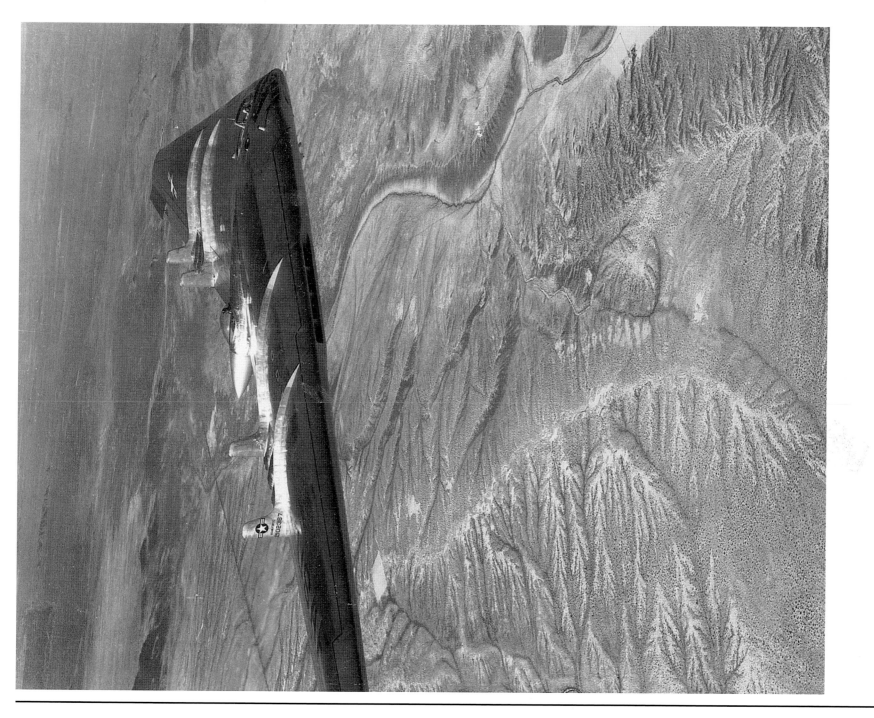

Jack Northrop's dream of a "clean" plane was nearly realized in the YB-49. Reduced drag and increased lift is the basis of this sleek aircraft. (Northrop)

The fences along the upper wing surface acted as a barrier to prevent spanwise flow of the boundary layer. The mechanical slots, which were sealed closed in high-speed flight, opened in the low-speed realm to delay stalls at higher angles of attack. (Northrop)

Last giant Northrop flying wing bomber of the XB-35/YB-49 family to take to the air was the YRB-49A. This six-jet photo-reconnaissance version had two of its jet engines placed in pylons under the wing in order to provide greater fuel space within the wing, for the purpose of increasing its range. (Northrop)

X-4

The XS-4 (later designated X-4) was a mid-1940s designed research aircraft built to investigate stability and control problems of a swept wing, tailless craft at transonic speeds. Two of these glossy white aircraft were built of which the first saw most of its service under the Northrop/Air Force test program while the second article flew most of the time with NACA. The flight test program showed that above Mach 0.76 the aircraft experienced constant yawing and rolling motions. At the same time, elevon effectiveness decreased considerably. At higher Mach numbers, uncontrollable oscillations about the three axes were encountered. Looking back, the results were not too surprising as the much earlier Messerschmitt Me 163 and de Havilland D.H. 108 Swallow experienced the same difficulties.

X-4 Statistics:

Northrop Specification:	NS-26
Number Produced and Flown:	2
Military Serial Numbers:	46-676 and 46-677
Wingspan:	26.83 ft.
Overall Length:	23.33 ft.
Overall Height:	14.83 ft.
Wing Area:	200 sq. ft.
Takeoff Weight:	7,500 lb.
Speed - Maximum:	680 mph
Speed - Cruising:	330 mph
Range:	320 miles
Service Ceiling:	44,000 ft.
Engines:	2 Westinghouse XJ-30-WE-7, 8

Above: The XS-4 (later redesignated X-4), like other aircraft of similar design (Me-163B-1 and DeHavilland D.H.108 Swallow) not only used the sweptback wing design for stability and control but also to delay drag rise and shock formation over the wing. Pictured here is the first, serial number 46-676, of two X-4 research aircraft produced. Below: Rear view of the tailless X-4 shows the exhaust for the two 1,600 lb. Westinghouse turbojet engines. Trailing edge controls consisted of outboard elevons and inboard split flaps which also acted as speed brakes and landing flaps. (both - Northrop)

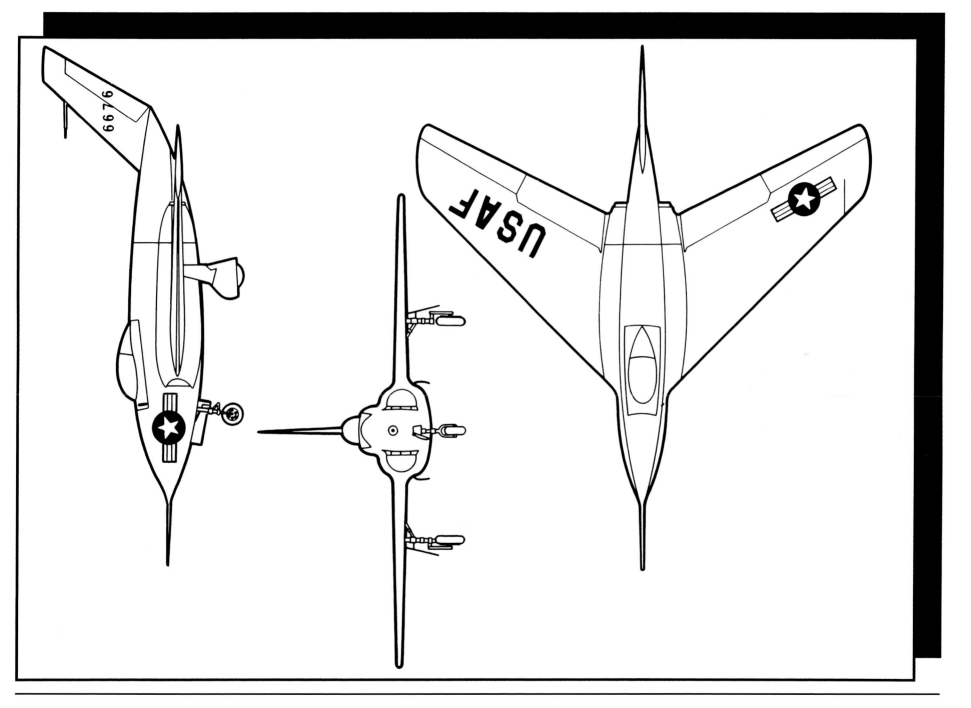

Northrop Test Pilot Charles Tucker in the cockpit of the No. 1 X-4 preparing for flight. The X-4 was painted over all white. (Northrop)

X-4, No.2 was flown under the National Advisory Committee for Aeronautics (NACA) control for most of its active career. The standard NACA yellow band and NACA emblem was later painted on the vertical stabilizer. Serial number 46-677 (Northrop)

N-25 and N-69 (SM-62) Snark

In answer to a late 1945 Army Air Forces request for guided missile research program proposals, Northrop responded with a proposal that would evolve into the Snark. This would be the last of the flying wing and tailless projects for Jack Northrop. With his resignation from his company in late 1952, the Northrop company would not be associated with a wing project for nearly 30 years. Jack Northrop would be one of the first Americans, outside of the small circle of engineers and scientists on the project, to learn of the Stealth bomber.

N-25 and N-69 Statistics:

Northrop Specification:	Numerous	
	N-25	N-69
Wingspan:	42.0 ft.	42.0 ft.
Overall Length:	52.0 ft.	69.0 ft.
Overall Height:	12.0 ft.	15.0 ft.
Wing Area:	280 sq. ft.	326 sq. ft.
Takeoff Weight:	28,000 lb.	60,000 lb.
Speed - Maximum:	Mach 0.9	Mach 0.9
Speed - Cruising:	Mach 0.85	Mach 0.85
Range:	6,000 miles	
Service Ceiling:	45,000 ft.	50,000+ ft.
Engines:	1 Pratt & Whitney	
	J-33	J-57
Armament:	5,000 lb. Warhead	

The square enclosure over the tail cone of this N-69D Snark contains a drag chute which is released by radio command from a missile director aircraft or a ground control station. These missiles were painted overall red with white stripping. (Northrop)

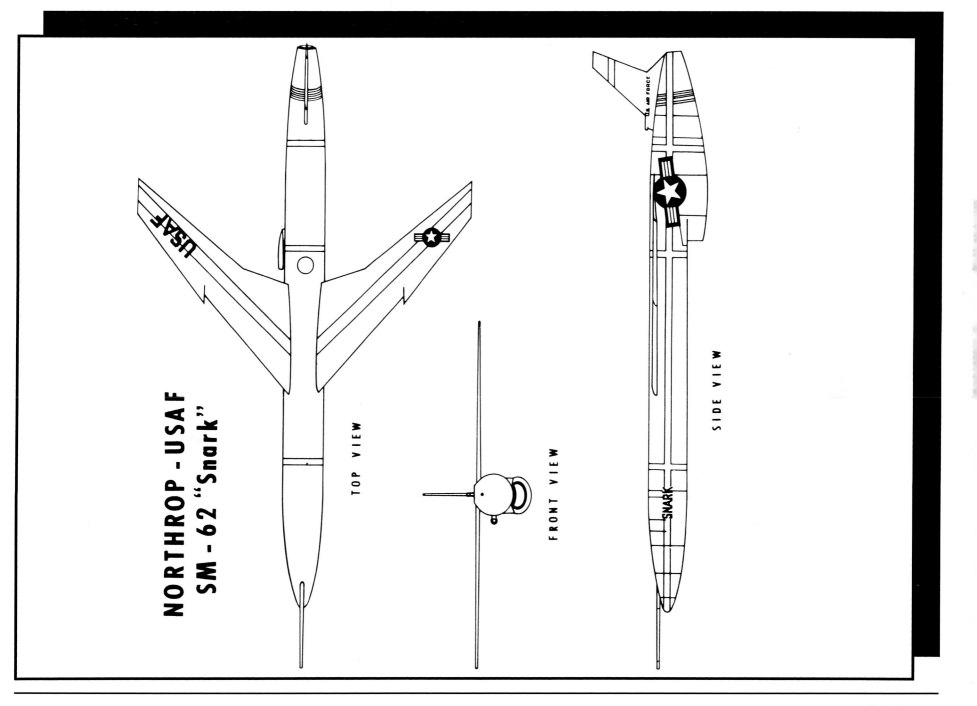

NORTHROP - USAF SM - 62 "Snark"

TOP VIEW

FRONT VIEW

SIDE VIEW

USAF

U.S. AIR FORCE

SNARK

F-89 Scorpion, flying as director aircraft with a Snark during the flight test program. First flight of the N-69 was on August 3, 1953. This was the last of the flying wing/ tailless craft to take to the air whose design had started under Jack Northrop's reign at Northrop Aircraft, Inc. (Northrop)

After ten years of development and testing, the SM-62 (Northrop N-69) started its service under Strategic Air Command (SAC) at Presque Isle in Maine. It never reached its potential due to continuing design problems. (Northrop)

QUEEN OF THE MIDNIGHT SKIES
The Story of America's Air Force Night Fighters

Garry R. Pape & Ronald C. Harrison

Detailed chronicle of American WWII night fighter program from its earliest conception to the end of the war, and covers all squadrons in Europe and the Pacific. Covers, development of radar, aircraft and modern air defenses.

Size: 8 1/2" x 11"   368 pages, over 700 b/w and color photographs, maps, squadron victory listing

ISBN: 0-88740-415-4   hard cover $45.00

Wright Flyer
Junkers J1
Fokker Dr.I
Junkers Ju 52
Polikarpov I-16
Messerschmitt Bf 109
Boeing B-17
Douglas DC-3/C-47
Messerschmitt Bf 110
Junkers Ju 88
Macchi MC.200-207
Messerschmitt Me 209
Nakajima Ki-43 Hayabusa
Lockheed P-38 Lightning
Heinkel He 178
Hawker Tornado/Typhoon
Ilyushin Il-2 Sturmovik
Arado Ar 240
Chance Vought F4U Corsair
North American P-51 Mustang
DeHavilland Mosquito
Messerschmitt Me 262
Hawker Tempest
Arado Ar 234
Dornier Do 335
Republic F-84F Thunderstreak
Hawker Hunter
North American F-100 Super Sabre
Lockheed F-104 Starfighter
Saab J35 Draken
Vought F-8 Crusader
Mikoyan/Gurevich MiG-21
Dassault-Breguet Mirage III/5
Northrop T-38 Talon
Hawker Siddeley Harrier
Dornier Do 31
Aérospatiale/BAC Concorde

Hans Redemann

INNOVATIONS IN AIRCRAFT CONSTRUCTION
Thirty-Seven Influential Designs

Hans Redemann

This superb study of thirty-seven aircraft that changed the course of aviation, explores development from the Wright Flyer to the Concorde.
Size: 8 1/2" x 11"   248 pages, over 300 b/w and color photographs, line drawings
ISBN: 0-88740-338-7   hard cover $29.95

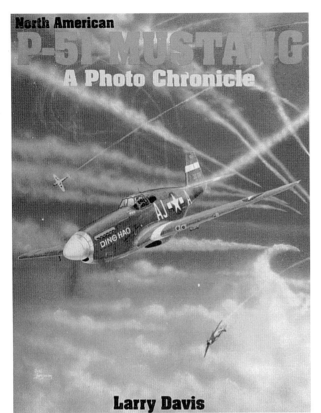

NORTH AMERICAN
P-51 Mustang
A Photo Chronicle

Larry Davis

The famed U.S. World War II fighter from the early B models to the P-82 Twin Mustang on all war fronts.
Size: 8 1/2" x 11"   112 pages, over 200 b/w and color photographs
ISBN: 0-88740-411-1   soft cover $19.95

LOCKHEED
F-94 Starfire
A Photo Chronicle

David R. McLaren/Marty Isham

The first U.S. night/all-weather fighter aircraft is chronicled, as is its use by Air Defense Command, Continental Air Command, and Alaska and North-East Air Command, and the Air National Guard.
Size: 8 1/2" x 11"   128 pages, over 220 b/w and color photographs
ISBN: 0-88740-451-0   soft cover $19.95

DOUGLAS
A-1 SKYRAIDER
A Photo Chronicle

Frederick A. Johnsen

The famed Skyraider in Korea and Vietnam, emphasizing its great ground assault capabilities.
Size: 8 1/2" x 11"   approx. 112 pages, over 100 b/w, and color photographs
ISBN: 0-88740-512-6   soft cover $19.95